Action Art

Making collage

Isabel Thomas

www.raintreepublishers.co.uk
Visit our website to find out more information about **Raintree** books.

To order:
 Phone 44 (0) 1865 888112
 Send a fax to 44 (0) 1865 314091
 Visit the Raintree Bookshop at **www.raintreepublishers.co.uk** to browse our catalogue and order online.

First published in Great Britain by Raintree, Halley Court, Jordan Hill, Oxford OX2 8EJ, part of Harcourt Education.
Raintree is a registered trademark of Harcourt Education Ltd.

Editorial: Melanie Copland, Kate Buckingham and Lucy Beevor
Design: Jo Malivoire and AMR
Picture Research: Mica Brancic
Production: Duncan Gilbert
Originated by Modern Age
Printed and bound in China by South China Printing Company

ISBN 1 844 21242 4 (hardback)
09 08 07 06 05
10 9 8 7 6 5 4 3 2 1

British Library Cataloguing in Publication Data
Thomas, Isabel
Making collage – (Action Art)
702.8'12

A full catalogue record for this book is available from the British Library.

Acknowledgements
Corbis p. 5; Getty p. 7 (The Image Bank); Harcourt Education pp. 4, 6, 9, 10, 11, 12, 13, 14, 15, 16, 17, 18, 19, 20, 21, 22, 23, 24, (Tudor Photography); Topfoto, p. 8 (The Image Works)

Cover photograph of collage reproduced with permission of Harcourt Education (Tudor Photography)

Every effort has been made to contact copyright holders of any material reproduced in this book. Any omissions will be rectified in subsequent printings if notice is given to the publishers.

The paper used to print this book comes from sustainable resources.

Some words are shown in bold, **like this**. You can find them in the glossary on page 23.

Contents

What is art?

Art is something you make when you are being **creative**.

People like to look at art.

A person who makes art is called an artist.

You can be an artist too!

How can
I create art?

There are lots of ways to create art.

You can draw and paint pictures.

You can make colourful sculptures and prints.

Collage is another kind of art.

What is collage?

Collage is making pictures by sticking different things on to paper or card.

Look at all the **materials** you can use to make collage.

How do I make collage?

Collect the **materials** that you want to use.

Cut big things into smaller pieces.

brush

glue

You can cut out shapes, too.

Use dabs of glue to stick the materials down.

What can I use to make collage?

You can tear paper into pieces.

Fold or scrunch the paper to give it **texture**.

Make collage with things that get thrown away.

You can **recycle** old **materials**.

What else can I use to make collage?

Fabric collage is nice to touch.

Cotton wool feels soft and fluffy.

Look for art **materials** in
the kitchen!

Try making collage with shiny foil
and pasta shapes.

What pictures can I make with collage?

cotton wool

leaves

paper

You can make a picture of something real.

This boy is making a collage of a garden.

You can make up shapes
and patterns.

This is called a design.

How does collage make me feel?

When you **display** your collage, you feel proud.

It is fun to talk about collage.

Say what the different **textures** feel like.

Let's make collage!

Let's make a snake collage!

1. Collect **materials** that look and feel interesting.

2. Cut fabric and paper into small pieces.

3. Draw the shape of a snake on a big piece of card. Draw stripes on the body.

4. Dab glue on to the first stripe. Stick on pieces of material.

5. Fill in each stripe with something different. Add eyes and a tongue, too.

Quiz

Look at these **materials**.

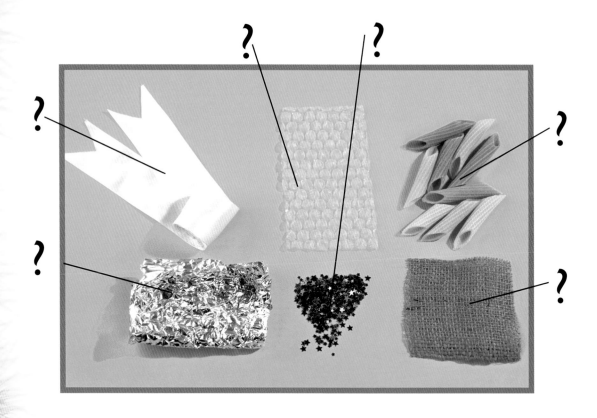

Which ones feel rough? Which ones feel smooth?

Look for the answers on page 24.

Glossary

 **creative** making something using your own ideas and how you feel inside

 **display** put your art where other people can look at it

 **materials** things you use to make art

 **recycle** use something that would be thrown away

 **texture** how something feels when you touch it

Index

Answers to quiz on page 22

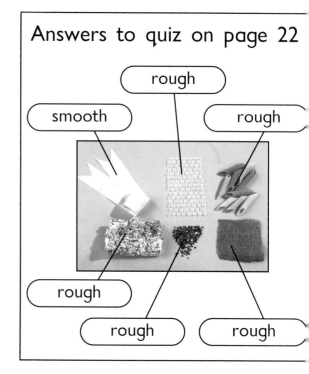

rough

smooth

rough

rough

rough

rough